Insects
&Spiders

SIMON & SCHUSTER BOOKS FOR YOUNG READERS
An imprint of Simon & Schuster Children's Publishing Division
1230 Avenue of the Americas, New York, New York 10020

Conceived and produced by Weldon Owen Pty Ltd
59-61 Victoria Street, McMahons Point
Sydney, NSW 2060, Australia

Copyright © 2008 Weldon Owen Pty Ltd

WELDON OWEN GROUP
Chairman John Owen

WELDON OWEN PTY LTD
Chief Executive Officer Sheena Coupe
Creative Director Sue Burk
Concept Development John Bull, The Book Design Company
Publishing Coordinator Mike Crowton
Senior Vice President, International Sales Stuart Laurence
Vice President, Sales and New Business Development Amy Kaneko
Vice President, Sales: Asia and Latin America Dawn Low
Administrator, International Sales Kristine Ravn

Project Editor Lachlan McLaine
Designer Terry Squadrito, Burk Design
Cover Designers Gaye Allen, Kelly Booth, Brandi Valenza
Design Assistant Sarah Norton
Art Manager Trucie Henderson
Illustrators Peter Bull Art Studio, Leonello Calvetti, *.tina Draempaehl,
Christer Eriksson, Steve Hobbs, MBA Studios, Jurgen Ziewe (The Art Agency)

Color reproduction by Chroma Graphics (Overseas) Pte Ltd
Printed by SNP Leefung Printers Ltd
Manufactured in China

A WELDON OWEN PRODUCTION

SIMON & SCHUSTER BOOKS FOR YOUNG READERS is a trademark of Simon & Schuster, Inc.
The text for this book is set in Meta and Rotis Serif.
10 9 8 7 6 5 4 3 2 1
Cataloging-in-publication data for this book is available from the Library of Congress.

ISBN-13: 978-1-4169-3868-2
ISBN-10: 1-4169-3868-0

Insects
&Spiders

Noel Tait

Simon & Schuster Books for Young Readers
New York   London   Toronto   Sydney

Contents

introducing

in focus

introducing

Antennae *These sensory organs help the insect to touch, hear, smell, and taste.*

Head *The head contains the main sensory organs, the brain, and the mouthparts. It is one of the strongest parts of the body.*

Ocelli *These simple eyes can detect the intensity and direction of light.*

Compound eyes *Adult insects have compound eyes made up of a large number of individual eyes packed together. They are good for detecting movement and give a wide field of vision.*

Thorax *The legs and wings are connected to the thorax. It contains the large muscles and nerves that control walking and flying.*

What Is an
Insect?

Insects are the most successful creatures on Earth. There are more kinds of insects than all other plant and animal species put together. Insects can be found almost everywhere: walking on the ground, burrowing in the soil, and flying in the air; from the polar regions to the tropics; in forests, grasslands, jungles, and deserts. Insects belong to a group of animals called arthropods, which also includes spiders, scorpions, crabs, and millipedes. Arthropods do not have an internal skeleton to support their body; instead, they have a tough outer shell called an exoskeleton. Insect bodies are divided into three basic parts—the head, thorax, and abdomen. All adult insects have three pairs of legs and most have wings.

A typical insect

Insects come in a huge variety of shapes and sizes, but they all share some common internal and external features. This illustration shows a European wasp, *Vespula germanica*. Below, the wasp's internal anatomy is revealed with its major organs color-coded.

Weighty in numbers

Although insects are small, if you put them all together on a scale, they would weigh more than all the other land animals on Earth.

Abdomen *This is the largest part of the body. It contains most of the vital organs.*

Reproductive system *Female insects have ovaries (illustrated) that produce huge numbers of eggs. The males have small testes that produce sperm.*

Venom gland *Wasp venom is a mixture of chemicals that can kill prey or drive away predators.*

Wings *Only adult insects have wings. Wasps, like most insects, have two pairs of wings that are folded against the body when not in use.*

Heart *Insects have no arteries or veins. Instead, blood fills the body cavity and supplies nutrients to the organs directly. The tubelike heart pumps blood around the body.*

Respiratory system *Insects breathe through air holes along the sides of the body called spiracles. These are connected to air sacs and fine tubes that take oxygen to all parts of the body.*

Tarsus

Claw

Digestive system *Food is passed quickly through the thorax and is digested in the midgut within the abdomen. Waste material is released as dry pellets and crystals of uric acid.*

Fungi (4.9%)

Bacteria (0.3%)

Other animals (19.9%)

Algae (1.9%)

Higher plants (17.6%)

Protozoa (2.2%)

Insects (53.2%)

Big slice of life

So far, about one and a half million species of living things have been identified and given a scientific name. Insects are by far the largest group, accounting for more than half of all named species. Only a small fraction of insect species have been properly identified, which means there are undoubtedly millions more.

Legs *Insect legs have five major segments. At the end of each leg is a flexible foot called the tarsus; a claw; and sometimes a sticky pad.*

Nervous system *The brain is connected to a nerve cord that extends along the underside of the body. It has a number of ganglia or "mini-brains" along its length that control activities in their part of the body.*

Salivary glands *These glands produce enzymes that lubricate and partially digest food.*

Insect Senses

Insects are active creatures that must quickly detect and respond to changes in their surroundings. Like us, insects have five main senses—sight, hearing, smell, touch, and taste. Their large, prominent eyes can detect shape, color, and especially movement. Insects' bodies are covered in hairs which are used to hear, touch, smell, and taste. The hairs on the antennae, mouthparts, and legs are particularly sensitive. For many insects, smell is very important in detecting food, which might be the nectar from fragrant flowers or foul-smelling feces or rotting flesh. Producing and detecting sounds and smells is a vital part of insect communication, particularly when it comes to mating.

Cone

Lens

Receptor cell

Optic nerve

Inside the eye *Compound eyes are made up of a large number of individual eyes. Each eye has a lens at the surface with a second conical lens inside. These lenses focus the light down a receptor cell that is connected to the optic nerve that leads to the brain. The brain then creates a composite image of the insect's world.*

Into the light

Night-flying moths are attracted to light—porch lights, car headlights, even the fatal flame of a candle or campfire. No one is sure why. Most likely, moths navigate by the Moon and other natural sources of light. Artificial lights confuse them and cause them to fly a spiraling course toward the light source.

Compound eye
The surface of the eye is a mosaic of the hexagonal lenses of individual eyes.

Proboscis *Most moths feed on nectar sucked through a strawlike proboscis that is covered with taste receptors. Moths can also taste food through receptors on their feet.*

Feathery sniffer *Moths that fly at night use their feathery antennae to locate flowers and mates. The male emperor moth has the best sense of smell of any animal. It can detect a female from a distance greater than 6 miles (10 km).*

Moving Around

Insects are among the most mobile of all animals. Some species are specialized for walking or running—their six jointed legs allow them to move fast while keeping stable. Because insects weigh so little, they can start, stop, and change direction much more suddenly than we can. But most insects prefer to fly. Flying is an effective way to escape from danger, find a mate, or search for food. For example, dragonflies fly so quickly, they can hunt other insects in the air. Most insects have two pairs of wings. Wings are thin, often transparent blades strengthened internally by rigid structures called veins. Insects can only fly once they have reached adulthood. As larvae, some insects swim in water; others, like fly maggots, wriggle around. Caterpillars walk on up to 16 legs. Ant and bee larvae do not need to move at all because their food is delivered to them. Some insects, such as silverfish, fleas, and lice, have no wings at all.

INSECTS ON THE MOVE

While the legs of most insects are designed for walking and running, some are adapted for moving in other ways.

Mole cricket *A mole cricket uses its powerful shovel-shaped front legs for tunneling underground.*

Water beetle *A water beetle's rear pair of legs are flattened and fringed with stout hairs. These legs are used as paddles and allow the beetle to dive below the surface of ponds.*

Inchworm *These caterpillars move by first pulling the abdomen toward the head to form a loop. The head end then reaches forward and the cycle is repeated.*

Flea *Inside a flea's large rear legs is an elastic material that stores energy like a spring. When it is released, the flea is catapulted upward and forward.*

3 **Airborne** *The ladybug releases its firm hold on the plant and begins to flap its wings. The wing case is shaped to provide lift in the air.*

Zigzagger

When an insect walks or runs, it always moves three legs at a time, forming a pattern of alternating tripods. The first and third legs of one side move together with the middle leg of the other side. This results in a slightly zigzagging walk.

1 Grounded *A ladybug spends most of its time walking on branches, leaves, and flowers, where it preys on other small insects. Its flight wings are usually packed away under its hardened wing case.*

Ladybug liftoff

Beetles like this ladybug have a hardened first pair of wings that form a protective covering over the delicate flight wings below. Many predators have difficulty penetrating this coat of armor.

2 Ready for launch *To launch itself into the air, the ladybug stands erect, opens its wing case, and unfurls its flight wings, ready for takeoff.*

The power to fly

In most flying insects, the flight muscles are attached to the inside wall of the thorax. Contractions from top to bottom cause the thorax to flatten, which drives the wings upward. Contractions from front to back cause the thorax to expand and drive the wings downward. Some insects, like butterflies, beat their wings only a few times per second, but midges are on the other end of the scale—they beat their wings an astonishing 1,000 times per second!

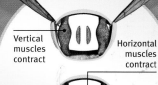

Vertical muscles contract

Horizontal muscles contract

Food and
Feeding

Most individual insects are quite picky about what they eat, but across all species, insects' diets vary widely, and there are few things dead or alive that they will not consume. More than half the world's insects are plant eaters. Any part of a plant might be eaten, from the leaves to the roots. Some insects tunnel inside a plant's tissue, which gives them both food and protection at the same time. Carnivorous insects feed on small animals, mostly other insects. Insects that suck the blood of animals or the sap of plants have a sharp proboscis to get through the skin or bark to the nutritious fluids below. Many insects specialize in eating decaying plant matter or the dead bodies of animals. Often an insect will do most of its eating at the larval stage of its life, while as an adult, it concentrates on reproduction.

Grace before dinner

Praying mantises are voracious carnivores—the lions of the insect world. When resting, they hold their forelegs together as if in prayer. But when prey ventures too close, these forelegs can be instantly transformed into lethal weapons as they snap shut in a deadly grip. Female praying mantises are also known to eat the male during or after mating.

PITFALL TRAP

Antlions are the larvae of insects called lacewings. They excavate a cone-shaped trap in fine sand and wait just below the surface. Ants that stumble into the pit cannot climb back out and are quickly seized in the antlion's enormous jaws. Ants that come close to the rim of the pit are knocked back down by sand kicked up by the waiting antlion.

Hawkmoth *The hawkmoth's rapid wingbeat allows it to hover like a hummingbird. It uses its extended proboscis to suck up nectar from deep within flowers.*

Caterpillar *Caterpillars are the larval stage of butterflies and moths. They feed on plants. They have hard, grinding jaws for chewing tough plant tissue.*

Cockroach *Cockroaches are not fussy about what they eat as long as it is not alive. Many species have invaded our homes, where they feed on food scraps.*

Bedbug *These insects hide in crevices during the day and emerge at night to suck the blood of humans and other warm-blooded animals. They usually feed just before dawn. Fortunately, they are not known to transmit disease.*

Reproduction and
Life Cycle

All insects begin life as eggs. After they hatch, young insects go through various life stages before they become adults. This process is called metamorphosis. From egg to adulthood, insects go through three or four stages depending on the species. While the life span of most adult insects is brief, they are mobile and can quickly find a mate. Insects use all their senses to locate individuals of the opposite sex. Often they will release a perfume, sing a love song, or perform a visual display to attract attention. After mating, the females often disperse to new habitats to lay their eggs.

Summer serenades
Male cicadas are the loudest insects in the world. They sing to attract females. The noise is made by vibrating membranes, called tymbals. The sound is amplified by air sacs in the abdomen.

Tymbal cover
Muscle
Tymbal membrane

BATTLE FOR A MATE

Male insects, like many other animals, often compete with each other for the right to mate with a female. Male stag beetles fight using their large antler-like jaws in much the same way as deer use their antlers. They rarely hurt each other badly. The loser usually just runs away.

Insect eggs

Insects are usually careful to lay their eggs in places that will give their larvae the best chance of survival. Apart from the eggshell, many eggs have additional coverings to protect them from the environment and predators.

Mosquito raft
Mosquitoes lay their eggs one at a time then stick them together to form floating rafts.

Cockroach egg case
As many as 50 cockroach eggs are laid together in a hard egg case.

Lacewing egg stalks
Lacewing eggs on long delicate stalks stay safely out of reach of small predators.

Bee egg
The colony queen lays a bee egg in each cell of the honeycomb.

Beetle eggs
Beetle eggs are often laid on the leaves that the larvae will later feed on.

An adult is born

Cicadas spend most of their lives—from 4 to 17 years depending on the species—as larvae in the soil. Apart from the lack of wings, the larvae, called nymphs, look similar to adults. The transformation from nymph to adult does not involve a complete bodily change. This is called incomplete metamorphosis. About 12 percent of insect species develop in this way.

1 **Egg** *Adult female cicadas lay clusters of eggs in grooves cut into a twig.*

4 **Adult** *The nymph climbs a tree trunk and molts one last time. The adult emerges from its shell, gradually unfurls its wings, and is ready for its brief life in the open air.*

2 **Nymph** *A newly hatched nymph drops to the ground and immediately buries itself in the soil.*

3 **Life underground** *The nymph feeds on sap by piercing roots with its needle-like mouthparts. After years underground, it eventually emerges from the soil.*

Metamorphosis

Many young insects look completely different from the adults they will become. For these insects, it is not just a matter of growing wings on reaching adulthood. Instead, most larval body parts are destroyed and new adult organs are developed—it is like having two animals in the same body. This dramatic and remarkable change is called complete metamorphosis. The transformation from larva to adult happens in a stage called the pupa. Unlike larvae, pupae do not eat and many cannot move. Many pupae form tough cases to protect themselves while they change. Others build silk or earth cocoons, or simply find a safe place to hide.

5 **Free to fly** *When its wings have unfurled and dried, the butterfly is ready to fly off in search of a mate.*

CHRYSALIS

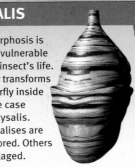

Metamorphosis is a very vulnerable stage in an insect's life. A caterpillar transforms into a butterfly inside a protective case called a chrysalis. Some chrysalises are brightly colored. Others are camouflaged.

Indian leaf
Kallima paralekta

Cloudless sulfur
Phoebis sennae

Paper kite
Idea leuconoe

1 **Eggs** *These are usually laid on or near the caterpillar's favorite food.*

2 **Caterpillar** *At the larval stage, the eggshell splits and the newly hatched caterpillar immediately begins to feed.*

3 **Pupa** *After growing and molting several times, the caterpillar attaches itself to a plant and pupates within its chrysalis.*

Time for a change

Insects that change completely when they mature have four stages in their life cycles. Each stage usually lasts for a different length of time and these times vary from species to species.

Stag beetle
The stag beetle is a relatively slow developer.

Ladybug
A ladybug spends over half its life as an adult.

Caddis fly
The caddis fly spends most of its short life as a larva.

| Key | Egg | Larva | Pupa | Adult | 0 | 1 | Years | 2 | 3 | 4 |

4 **Emergence** *After a few weeks the chrysalis splits and the butterfly slowly emerges.*

A complete makeover

The blue morpho butterfly has four stages in its life cycle—egg, larva, pupa, and adult. The transformation of a larval caterpillar into a butterfly is one of the wonders of nature.

Insects

In the Water

Many insects live all or part of their lives in water. Some species can tolerate salty water, but most aquatic insects need freshwater. Some insects spend only their larval stages in water, while others are totally aquatic at all stages of their lives. Aquatic insects have features that allow them to swim and breathe underwater. These features can look and function a lot like those things humans have invented to spend time underwater, such as the flippers, snorkels, and air tanks used by scuba divers. Just as we do, most aquatic insects eventually have to come to the surface to breathe air. But some have developed gills that allow them to stay underwater permanently.

Watery world

Aquatic insects are found in lakes, ponds, rivers, and creeks. Some live at the surface of the water, while others swim about underwater. Many live on the muddy bottom, sheltering under stones or among the water plants for protection. Remarkably, five known species of water striders spend their lives on the ocean surface.

Mating A male (top) and female dragonfly come together to mate. Gripping the female just behind her head, the male fertilizes her eggs.

Diving beetle *Diving beetles catch their prey with their strong front legs. They take a bubble of air under their wings when they dive so that they can breathe underwater.*

Mosquito larvae *Mosquito larvae swim by wriggling their body back and forth. They regularly swim to the surface to breathe through a snorkel at the back end of the body.*

Whirligig beetle *Whirligig beetles constantly swim in circles on the surface of ponds in search of prey. Their bodies are shaped like canoes and their legs work like paddles.*

Dragonfly eggs *Dragonfly eggs are coated with a type of jelly that secures them to water plants and keeps them from being swept away.*

Caddis fly larvae *Caddis fly larvae protect themselves by building cases from plant stems and sand grains bound together with silk.*

Mosquito pupae *Mosquito pupae come to the surface headfirst because at this stage their snorkel is up front. They are called tumblers because of the jerky way they swim.*

Dragonfly larvae *These ferocious predators stalk their prey. When they get close enough, they shoot out a hinged jaw from their lower lip. The jaw has sharp hooks on the end that spear the prey.*

Staying Alive

Insects are so numerous and nutritious that it is no surprise plenty of other creatures are out to eat them. In response, insects have evolved an amazing variety of strategies to avoid predators. Spider webs are designed to capture flying insects, so butterflies and moths have developed wings covered in loose scales that stick to the web, allowing the insects themselves to escape. Some insects use camouflage or mimicry to protect themselves, whereas others are poisonous or taste bad. These insects are often brightly colored as a warning not to eat them. Other insects take a more active approach, biting with strong jaws, stinging, or squirting acid to ward off attackers. Some, such as mayflies, are essentially defenseless, but they exist in such enormous numbers that millions can be eaten without threatening the survival of the species.

Off with a bang

When a bombardier beetle is threatened, it combines chemicals in a chamber at the tip of its abdomen. The result is an explosive chemical reaction and a deadly spray of boiling-hot noxious fluid and gas. The beetle has a highly mobile abdomen and can direct its spray with great accuracy.

Gland *These paired glands produce a powerful toxin and hydrogen peroxide, which form the basis for the exploding mixture.*

Reservoir *The chemicals are stored, ready for action, in the two reservoirs.*

Muscle *These muscles control the valves leading from the reservoirs to the explosion chamber.*

Glands *These produce enzymes that force oxygen from hydrogen peroxide within the explosion chamber.*

Explosive chamber *This chamber has rigid walls that force the chemicals and hot gas outward with an audible bang.*

CAMOUFLAGE AND MIMICRY

One of the best methods of defense is not to be noticed in the first place, so many insects are brilliantly camouflaged. Others are mimics, meaning they look like something a predator would not be interested in eating.

Eyed hawkmoth *If this camouflaged dull-colored moth is detected, it quickly opens its wings to reveal a menacing pair of eye spots that scare away potential predators.*

Leaf mimic katydid *The color and form of this katydid's wing covers give it the appearance of a dry leaf.*

Stick insect *A long, narrow body and legs, together with statue-like posture, make this insect look just like a stick or twig.*

Bark bug *A resting bark bug is almost invisible against the trunk of a tree, thanks to its flat body, color, and texture.*

Orchid mantis *This mantis disguises itself as an orchid flower to avoid potential predators. It also fools insect prey that visit to collect nectar.*

Cooperative
Insects

Most insects are loners that come together only to mate with another insect, but some insects have a very different way of life. Cooperative insects band together to form incredibly complex societies called colonies. Within these insect colonies there are several castes. Each caste has special duties to perform for the benefit of the whole colony. Castes can include males and females as the fertile reproducers, soldiers to defend the colony, and workers that carry out all other activities. All the members of a colony are related and no individual can live independently or join another colony. Cooperative insects have to be excellent communicators to ensure that they function efficiently. All ant and termite species, and many bees and wasps, are social insects.

Back to base *Foraging workers return to the hive laden with nectar in their stomach and pollen attached to their back legs.*

NESTS

Cooperative insects need a place to live together. Many species construct their own nests, while others burrow into the ground or into wood. Army ants do not have a permanent home. They can create a temporary nest from their interlinked bodies.

Hornet's nest *Wasp and hornet nests are made of mud or chewed plant matter that forms a paper-like material.*

Ant nest *Some ants build mounds that project above ground.*

Sun

Dance path

Direction to fly

Food source

Egg *The queen deposits a single egg into each cell.*

Waggle dance
Returning scout bees tell other workers where to find food with an elaborate figure-eight dance. The dance indicates the direction of food in reference to the Sun's position while the intensity of the "waggle" of the bee's abdomen indicates the distance.

Queen bee *The queen produces up to 2,500 eggs a day and lives for three to four years.*

Nursery duty *Nurse workers take nectar from the foragers and partially digest it to make honey to feed the developing larvae.*

Hive of activity

A beehive has a single queen that produces eggs from which all other members of the colony develop. Most of these will be workers that live for about two weeks. They first carry out domestic duties within the hive, feeding the larvae and molding the wax to form the cells that comprise the hive. After this, they leave the hive to forage for food.

Drone *Drones are male bees whose main job is to fertilize the new queen of a colony, after which they die. Drones develop from unfertilized eggs when required.*

Larva *A larva will develop into a queen if it is fed on a diet solely of royal jelly, a secretion from a gland in the head of workers. Workers develop from larvae fed partly on royal jelly and partly on honey and pollen.*

Pupa *A larva develops into a pupa before becoming an adult bee.*

Honey *Honey nectar that has been processed by nurse workers is fed to larvae and stored as food for adult bees over winter.*

Capped cell *After the larva changes into a pupa, the cell is sealed with wax.*

GOOD THINGS FROM INSECTS

Bees and silkworm moths are the only insects that have been domesticated by humans. Silk fabric is made from the cocoons of silkworm pupae, while bees provide us with honey and wax. Bees and other insects that collect nectar also pollinate the flowering plants that form an important part of our diet.

Silk kimono

Wax candles

Edible witchetty grub

Pollination

Honey

Insects and Us

When people think of insects, they tend to think first of the trouble insects bring, and it is true that insects can make life difficult. Insects compete with us for food and take advantage of our crops and food kept in storage. They can destroy our clothes and even our homes. Some insects are parasites; others transmit diseases that cause untold suffering and death. The stings of wasps, bees, and ants are painful, and repeated contact may result in fatal allergic reactions. However, insects also bring huge benefits. They constitute the diet of a large number of other animals and are an essential link in the food chain. Some pollinate plants or enrich the soil by breaking down organic material. Predatory insects keep pest numbers down. Some insects even make tasty snacks.

Mosquito menace

A mosquito's proboscis, consisting of a bundle of sharp feeding tubes, is strong enough to pierce skin. As the proboscis penetrates, the protective sheath around it folds back to allow the tubes to reach the blood below. In many parts of the world mosquitoes carry serious diseases from one human to another and a bite can end up being deadly.

Trouble inside *The malaria parasite, Plasmodium, is a single-celled microbe that infects red blood cells and the liver. When a mosquito feeds on the blood of an infected person, it also takes up the parasite. The disease is transmitted when the mosquito next bites an uninfected person.*

Sheath

Proboscis

What Is a
Spider?

Spiders can be found almost anywhere on Earth, except for the oceans and polar regions. They live both above and below the ground, on mountaintops, and even underwater. Like insects, spiders are arthropods. They belong to a group called the arachnids, which also includes scorpions, harvestmen, mites, and ticks. Arachnids have two parts to their body: the cephalothorax—a combined head and thorax—and the abdomen. They can easily be distinguished from insects because they have four pairs of legs and no antennae. Unlike other arachnids, spiders have a narrow waist between the cephalothorax and abdomen, and poisonous fangs. All spiders are carnivorous and feed largely on insects, which they either hunt or trap in sticky silken webs.

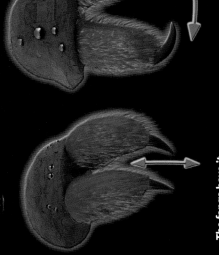

The fangs have it
Spiders can be divided into two groups. The hairy mygalomorphs (left) include tarantulas, trapdoor spiders, and their relatives. They have fangs that strike downward. The second group, araneomorphs (right), have fangs that strike sideways toward the center. More than 90 percent of spiders are araneomorphs.

Spider eye
A typical spider eye is a fairly simple organ consisting of a lens that covers a cup-shaped retina. Jumping spiders are an exception. They have an extended pair of eyes that function like telescopes, providing a sharp magnified image.

Venom gland The two salivary glands have been adapted to produce paralyzing venom.

Brain The top part is connected to the eyes. The lower part connects with the rest of the body.

Sucking stomach Food is sucked into this muscular organ and then moved along to the rest of the digestive tract.

Heart The heart is long and thin, and runs along the top of the abdomen.

Book lung Oxygen for the spider to breathe enters through this organ.

Ovary The female's eggs are produced in this organ.

Midgut Food is broken down in the midgut. From there, it passes into the bloodstream.

Silk gland This produces liquid silk which is pumped into the spinnerets.

Spinnerets Silk emerges from the small nozzles on the spinnerets.

Inside and out

Spiders come in many different sizes, but they all have the same basic shape. Most of the internal organs are concentrated in the abdomen. Unlike insects, spiders have silk glands and breathe through book lungs, not spiracles. This is a female mouse spider (*Missulena occatoria*) from Australia.

Eyes *Most spiders have eight simple eyes. They are arranged in many different patterns depending on the species. Despite having so many eyes, most spiders cannot see very well.*

Legs *Each leg has seven segments that provide great flexibility for moving about. They are very sensitive to vibrations.*

Fangs *Spiders use their jaws for attack and defense, and sometimes for digging burrows. Each jaw ends in a hollow fang that releases venom.*

Pedipalps *Spiders use these leglike body parts to touch and taste. During mating, males transfer sperm through the pedipalps.*

Claws *Spiders use these to cling on to rough surfaces. Web-building spiders have specially adapted claws that cling onto silk.*

Cephalothorax *This part of the body is protected above by a hard plate called the carapace. The feeding structures around the mouth are at the front and the legs radiate out from the sides.*

Abdomen *The abdomen is covered in a soft but tough skin, like leather. It contains most of the body organs and can expand in females as the ovary becomes full of eggs.*

Webmasters

Silk is one of the most amazing substances in nature and it plays an important role in the life of all spiders. Silk is not just for making webs—it can be used to wrap up prey, protect eggs, build a shelter, or serve as a safety line. This versatile substance is produced as a liquid inside a spider's silk glands, which open onto one to three pairs of spinnerets at the end of the abdomen. When the liquid silk is drawn out by the back pair of legs, it forms very fine but strong fibers. Spider silk is almost as strong as steel wire of the same width. Some silks are elastic and can be stretched to three times their length before breaking. Spiders can produce as many as eight types of silk, each for a different purpose.

Spinnerets *The tip of each spinneret is covered in tiny nozzles called spigots. The silk is squeezed out of the spigots to form fine fibers that quickly combine in a single thread. The spinnerets are mobile and can knit different types of silk together.*

Fly-fishing

Orb-weavers are a family of spiders that build the familiar spiral-shaped webs found in gardens, fields, and forests all over the world. Most species build their webs at night and hide during the day. Others are active both day and night. Building a web is hard work. Afterward, the spider conserves energy and waits patiently for an insect to fly into its sticky trap.

Sticky situation *This fly has become entangled in the sticky spiral threads of the web. As it struggles, vibrations are sent up the radial threads to the spider waiting at the hub. In an instant, the spider rushes to the prey to inject venom and then wrap it in silk to be dealt with later.*

How to build an orb web

1 A strong horizontal line is anchored at each end. Then the first two radial spokes are added to form the hub.

2 A stabilizing frame is added around the circumference, anchored at several points. Then more radials are added.

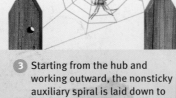

3 Starting from the hub and working outward, the nonsticky auxiliary spiral is laid down to connect the radials.

4 Using the auxiliary spiral as a guide, the sticky catching spiral is laid down. The auxiliary spiral is demolished in the process.

WEB TYPES

The conspicuous orb web is the most familiar type of web, but it is only one of many kinds that spiders make.

Hammock web *This web traps insects in a maze of vertical threads. They eventually fall onto a platform, where they are snatched by the waiting spider.*

Triangle web *This spider forms a bridge between the web and an attachment thread. On contact with prey, it lets go of the web, causing it to collapse.*

Scaffold web *The scaffold web has sticky vertical threads that are anchored to the ground to trap insects that walk by.*

Food parcel *After an orb-weaver spider catches a fly, it injects it with saliva and wraps it in silk. The spider cannot eat until the saliva has dissolved the fly's internal organs, forming a liquid "soup" that can be sucked out.*

Leg *Orb spiders have a middle claw that they use for walking on the nonsticky radial threads of the web. This claw hooks over the thread and locks it against a row of barbed bristles projecting from the underside of the claw.*

Little Killers
The Hunters

Not all spiders catch their prey with webs. Many species actively go out in search of their next meal. Some of these hunting spiders take advantage of the darkness of night, while some spiders hunt during the day. Others are ambush predators. They blend in with their surroundings and wait patiently for prey to come close enough to grab. Although hunting spiders can see better than web-building spiders, most rely primarily on vibration sensors and touch to detect prey. They respond with lightning speed. They grab the prey with their forelegs, pull it toward their gaping fangs, and then kill and subdue it with injected venom. It is all over in a fraction of a second. Many hunting spiders have tufts of hairs on their feet that make them more surefooted. Some can even walk on windows and ceilings with ease.

Gone fishing
A raft spider waits by the edge of a pond with its front legs touching the water. When it detects ripples coming from an insect larva, tadpole, or small fish, it runs across the surface of the pond to catch its prey.

EYE SPY

Hunting spiders usually have eight simple eyes placed around the carapace. The simple eyes are good for detecting movement in all directions. The arrangement and size of the eyes help indicate how a hunting spider gets its food.

Huntsmen *These agile hunters have all-around vision and can move quickly in any direction to grab prey.*

Ogre-faced spiders *These night hunters have two huge eyes that are hundreds of times more sensitive to light than our eyes.*

Crab spiders *These ambush hunters have good close-up vision for grabbing prey when it comes near.*

Flower traps

Crab spiders camouflage themselves among flowers. When an insect visits to collect nectar, the spider strikes in an instant. Like a chameleon, a crab spider can change its color to match its surroundings.

Fangs of the forest

Goliath bird-eating spiders live in the rain forests of northern South America. They spend most of their time in burrows but venture out to stalk then pounce on insects; small vertebrates such as frogs, lizards, and mice; and the occasional bird. They are the largest spiders in the world.

Spider
Defense

Spiders—aggressive, venomous predators—are in turn preyed on by a number of animals, including insects, frogs, lizards, birds, and mammals. But the main predators of spiders are other spiders. Spiders are usually secretive animals that remain motionless and hide in crevices and burrows, under bark, or within curled-up leaves. They emerge briefly only to hunt or find a mate, often under cover of darkness. Some spiders live in the open, protected by the barrier formed by their web. Others have sharp spines and bright warning colors. Still others camouflage themselves in order to remain undetected. Active spiders can defend themselves by rapidly escaping out of harm's way. In many instances, the strategies that allow spiders to evade predators also help spiders trap unwary prey.

SPIDER CAMOUFLAGE

Many spiders are masters of camouflage, which makes them difficult to detect in their natural environment. Other spiders may remain exposed, but their appearance mimics something foul-tasting or even dangerous to intended predators.

Wasp-mimicking spider *The long spinnerets on this spider's abdomen resemble the antennae on the head of a wasp, while this spider's head looks like a wasp's abdomen.*

Crab spider *If under threat, this spider rapidly drops to the ground, where it remains motionless and undetected until the danger has passed.*

Bird dung spiders *These spiders mimic bird droppings. A disagreeable smell completes the illusion.*

Wrap-around spider *The color, texture, and posture of this spider make it almost impossible to distinguish from a knot on an old tree trunk.*

Fast getaway

While many animals roll themselves
into a ball in response to danger, this
dune spider (*Carparachne aureoflava*)
takes the shape of the greatest of
all human inventions: the wheel. To
escape from a pompilid wasp, it flips
onto its side and literally cartwheels
down a steep sand dune.

Spider safety lines

When threatened, many spiders drop
quickly out of sight on a strong line
of silk called a dragline. The hind
legs reel out the dragline to regulate
the speed of descent.

Spider Life

Female spiders lay their eggs a few weeks after mating. Some species lay just a few eggs at a time, but others can lay 1,000 or more. All spiders wrap their eggs in a protective silk cocoon called an egg sac. Unlike insects, spiders hatch from eggs as miniature versions of the adults. As they grow bigger, they periodically have to shed their old exoskeletons in a process called molting. Spiders do not go through a metamorphosis in order to become a mature adult. Males become adults earlier than females and hence they are generally smaller. Apart from their size, males can be easily identified because they have enlarged tips to their pedipalps that look like boxing gloves. However, they are not used in combat but to transfer sperm to the female during mating.

Up, up, and away

One of a spiderling's first tasks in life is to get away from its siblings so it does not have to compete for food or risk being cannibalized. Some species do this by ballooning. Spiderlings face into the wind and release a thread of silk that is caught in the slightest breeze. In this way, they can fly thousands of feet into the air and travel hundreds of miles.

MOTHER LOVE

Most spiders play no part in caring for their offspring other than wrapping them up in a protective egg sac. However, some show maternal behavior, ranging from defending the egg sacs to caring for the hatched spiderlings.

Piggyback *A female wolf spider carries her egg sac around with her. When the spiderlings hatch, she opens the egg sac with her fangs. The spiderlings climb up her legs and hold tightly to the hairs on her abdomen.*

Feeding on mother *While it is rare for spiders to feed their offspring, some give their brood prey or regurgitate liquid food for them. This velvet spider nourishes her brood with her own dead body—the ultimate maternal sacrifice.*

Spider Life ◄ 37

Spider courtship

Because spiders are predators, the smaller males have to be cautious when approaching a potential mate. Male spiders have developed elaborate courtship rituals to ensure that the female does not think of him as her next meal.

Gift for the bride
The male nursery-web spider courts the female with an insect, gift-wrapped in silk. If she is willing, he mates with her while she is consuming the bridal meal.

Good vibrations
The web of a female orb-web spider is a dangerous place for any small creature to approach. The dwarf male strums a special signal on a thread to entice her down from the web.

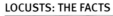

Locator map This map of the world shows you where the featured insect or spider is located. Look for the orange shading on each map.

LOCUSTS: THE FACTS

HABITAT: **Hot, dry areas**

DIET: **Plant material, particularly grasses**

SIZE: **0.4 inch (10 mm) to 4 inches (100 mm) long**

ILLUSTRATED SPECIES: *Schistocerca gregaria* **(Africa, Middle East, and Asia)**

Fast facts Fast facts at your fingertips give you essential information about the insect or spider featured.

Size comparison This shows the size of the insect or spider compared to a human hand.

Species bar This bar shows which category the specimen belongs to.

MONARCH BUTTERFLY: THE FACTS

HABITAT: Forests and open woodland

DIET: Milkweed (caterpillar); nectar (adult)

SIZE: 4 inch (10 cm) wingspan

SCIENTIFIC NAME: *Danaus plexippus*

Monarch

Butterfly

Migration is one of the most awe-inspiring events in nature. The numbers of individuals involved and the distances they travel can be enormous. For animals that live in regions with extreme seasonal change, there are two survival options: cope with the harsh climate at home or migrate to more favorable conditions elsewhere. In many cases, migration also gives newborns a better chance of survival. While many fish, birds, and mammals make long migrations, the monarch butterfly's journey of up to 2,200 miles (3,500 km) is all the more heroic because of the insect's size and fragility. It is also a great mystery. The butterflies that return south in fall are often the great-great-grandchildren of the butterflies that left in the spring, and yet somehow they are able to find their way back to the very same grove of trees.

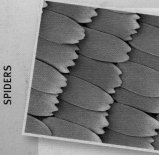

A closer look
The intricate design of a monarch butterfly can be seen only through a microscope.

Funny face Monarch butterflies have large compound eyes that help them find flowers to feed on and milkweed to lay their eggs on. When uncoiled, the proboscis is used like a straw to suck up nectar.

Wing scales The wings of butterflies and moths are covered with overlapping scales. Color patterns are made from pigments within the scales and the refraction of light as it bounces off fine ridges on the scales' surfaces.

Western range *Monarch butterflies west of the Rocky Mountains spend winter along the California coast.*

MONARCH LIFE CYCLE

It takes about one month for a monarch egg to develop into a butterfly. The eggs hatch into caterpillars with distinctive yellow, black, and white stripes. They grow quickly and are ready to pupate after about two weeks. The distinctive wing colors can be seen through the cocoon case just before the adult butterfly emerges.

1 Eggs on a milkweed leaf.
2 A caterpillar feeds.
3 The pupal stage.
4 An adult emerges from the cocoon.

Mighty migration

Most monarch butterflies live short adult lives of two to six weeks in the summer feeding grounds as far north as Canada. But those born in late summer are different. These butterflies make the epic journey south where they rest over the winter in the mountains near Mexico City. Next spring they mate and start the return journey north, before laying their eggs and finally dying at the age of about eight months.

Milkweed Monarch butterflies lay their eggs on milkweed because it is the only food that monarch caterpillars can eat. Milkweed contains a toxin that makes the adult butterfly poisonous if eaten.

C A N A D A

Key

● Eastern wintering grounds — ▷ Generation 1
○ Eastern summer grounds — ▷ Generation 2
● Western wintering grounds — ▷ Generation 3
○ Western summer grounds — ▷ Generation 4

M E X I C O

HOUSEFLY: THE FACTS

HABITAT: **Associated with humans**

DIET: **Dead and decaying plant and animal matter, feces**

SIZE: **0.3 inch (8 mm) long**

SCIENTIFIC NAME: *Musca domestica*

Uninvited Guest
Housefly

Houseflies are one of the most commonly encountered of all insects. Originally from central Asia, houseflies have spread, along with humans, all over the world. Houseflies are found everywhere humans are, particularly in houses and around farms. Female houseflies can lay up to a thousand eggs during their life of about two to three weeks. Eggs hatch into wormlike larvae, called maggots, that feed and grow. They eventually burrow into soil to form pupae, from which the adult emerges. The journey from egg to adult can take less than three weeks, which is why large numbers of flies can build up in summer. Some larvae and pupae survive the winter in protected locations and develop into adults as soon as warm weather returns in early summer.

Death in a can
Home insecticides are a big business. Most brands of fly spray contain pyrethrin, a natural insecticide that is extracted from chrysanthemum flowers. Pyrethrin damages the normal function of an insect's nervous system. It is effective at doses that will not harm birds or mammals.

Gripper *To hang on to rough surfaces, houseflies use a pair of claws at the tips of their legs. Between the claws there is a sticky pad that allows houseflies to walk on smooth surfaces like glass or even upside down on the ceiling.*

View from above
Houseflies belong to a group of insects called Diptera. Most flying insects have two pairs of wings, but Diptera have only one pair. The hind wings are tiny, clublike structures that help the fly balance when it is in the air.

Super vision *The housefly's large reddish brown eyes are sensitive to movement, enabling the fly to take off at the first sign of danger.*

Wing *When not flying, the transparent wings are folded over the back of the body.*

Proboscis *When not being used to feed, this organ is normally retracted inside the housefly's head.*

Leg *The front legs are not just for walking— they are used to taste food as well. Flies regularly rub their front legs together to keep them clean.*

Sucker *The tip of the proboscis acts like a sponge to soak up liquid food that is then sucked into the body. Flies liquefy solid food by vomiting acidic saliva onto it.*

Sweet treat

Houseflies feed and lay their eggs on garbage and feces. Because they are also attracted to human food, they are capable of spreading bacterial diseases such as food poisoning, typhoid, cholera, and dysentery.

This means war *Soldiers are specially adapted to fend off invaders, such as ants. In some termite species, the soldiers have large heads armed with formidable jaws. In others, the soldiers have a snout that ejects a sticky fluid at the intruders.*

Cooling shafts *Warm air rises into the chimneylike central shaft and is removed by the wind-driven outflow of air on the downwind side of the mound.*

TERMITES: THE FACTS

HABITAT: **Forests, grasslands, and human dwellings**

DIET: **Dead plant material, fungus**

SIZE: **0.1 inch (3 mm) to 1 inch (25 mm)**

ILLUSTRATED SPECIES: *Macrotermes michaelseni* (Africa)

Tower Builders
Termites

Like ants and bees, termites are social insects, which means they form colonies that contain anywhere from a few hundred to millions of insects. The members of a colony are born into groups, called castes, that each perform different tasks. Termites eat a variety of dead plant material, from small leaves, twigs, and grass to the giant trunks of fallen trees. Many species are considered pests because they eat the timber in our houses. They are one of the most efficient recyclers of cellulose, the major component of the hard fibers in plants. Termites are often called "white ants," because they superficially resemble ants in appearance and habits. In fact, they are more closely related to cockroaches and mantids.

BREATHING TOWER

The mound makes use of wind energy to breathe. It is shaped so that air pressure acting on the porous surface of the mound is not equal on all sides. Stale air is sucked out of the mound on the downwind side. Fresh air is drawn in from the upwind side.

Key ▲ Fresh air ▲ Stale air

Royal chamber This is the nursery of the colony. The queen's only job is to produce massive numbers of eggs—up to 2,000 a day. The king mates with her to fertilize her eggs. Workers attend to the royal pair and nurture the eggs and newly hatched nymphs.

Fungus farming Cellulose is difficult for animals to digest and many herbivores use bacteria and other microbes in their guts to help them do this. Some termites cultivate fungus that predigests the collected wood. This is done in special high-humidity chambers.

Cellar The cellar helps to control temperature and humidity in the mound. Workers dig shafts more than 125 feet (38 m) below the cellar to tap underground reserves of borewater.

Architecture by instinct

A few termite species, particularly in Africa and Australia, build impressive mounds aboveground. Constructed from soil mixed with saliva, the mounds are built by millions of blind worker termites and can reach 20 feet (6 m) high. The central part of the mound is where the termite activity is concentrated, while the rest is a maze of ventilation shafts.

Worker

Soldier

King

Queen

Termite castes
As with other social insects, there are several castes within a termite colony. Each has distinctive physical features and particular jobs to perform.

4 **Adult emerges** *The adult beetle eventually eats its way out of the dung and digs its way to the surface.*

5 **The cycle continues** *The adult flies off to seek a mate and more dung on which to feed.*

3 **Pupal stage** *When the larva has fully grown, it stops feeding and develops into the pupa, still within the protection of the dung ball.*

Dung beetle breeding

There are two main types of breeding behavior in dung beetles. Most species are "tunnelers"; they build a breeding nest directly underneath a dung pile. The more familiar "rollers" shape dung into balls. The male-and-female pair then roll the dung ball away in a straight line over any obstacle in their path until the beetles find a patch of soft soil in which to bury it.

2 **Feeding time** *The soft-bodied larva hatches from the egg and grows by eating the dung from the inside of the dung ball.*

Life's a Ball

Dung Beetle

Dung beetles feed almost exclusively on feces, which is commonly called dung. By swiftly removing dung and spreading it underground where it acts as a fertilizer, dung beetles provide a great service to the environment. Dung beetles help restrict the number of irritating and disease-carrying insect pests, such as flies, that also feed on dung. They belong to the large beetle family called scarabs. Most species come from Africa, where there are many large herbivorous mammals, such as elephants, buffalo, and giraffes. These animals produce huge quantities of dung, so the beetles are never short of a good meal. Adult beetles have soft mouthparts and feed only on the fluid part of the dung, leaving the fibrous part to be stored away for the larvae to eat.

1 **Get the ball rolling** *It is usually the male who provides the force to roll the large ball of dung; the female will often hitch a ride on top. The males also have to fight off other males who try to steal it. The female's job is to deposit an egg inside the ball once it is in the burrow.*

Ancient Egyptian scarab
Dung beetles were sacred to the ancient Egyptians. They symbolized the god Khepri, who was thought to roll the sun across the sky each day just as the dung beetle rolls its ball.

TARANTULA HAWK WASP: THE FACTS

HABITAT: **Rain forests to deserts**

DIET: **Nectar and fruit (adults); large spiders (larvae)**

SIZE: **0.5 inch (14 mm) to 2 inch (50 mm) long**

ILLUSTRATED SPECIES: *Pepsis formosa*
(southwestern United States)

Tarantula
Hawk Wasp

A female tarantula hawk wasp is a tarantula's worst nightmare. But she is not interested in eating spiders or even in killing them—she has something much worse in mind. This wasp uses the spider's living but paralyzed body as an incubator and food source for her young. The male wasps are also aggressive but only to other male wasps. They stake out a territory and defend it against other males. The sting of these large, robust wasps is among the most painful of any insect. Their dark blue body, often with contrasting orange-red wings, provides a warning of danger to others. Despite their aggressive nature, adult wasps are vegetarians that feed on nectar and fruit.

1 **The battle begins** *A female tarantula hawk wasp uses her sense of smell to hunt for spiders. When she locates a burrow, she will either entice the spider out into the open or enter the burrow and expel it. Often the bewildered spider's only defense is to rear up in a threatening posture.*

Giant slayer

Tarantula hawk wasps are only about half the size of their prey, but they are agile and strong. Once targeted, a tarantula has virtually no chance of escape.

5 **Pupa** *Having sated its appetite, the larva pupates. Finally a wasp, not a spider, emerges from the tarantula's burrow.*

4 **Larva** *After a few days the larva hatches from the egg, pierces the skin of the spider and begins to suck out its body juices. Eventually, the almost fully grown larva climbs into the body of the spider and eats the remaining vital organs. The spider is now dead.*

3 **Egg** *The paralyzed, but still living, spider is dragged down into its own burrow, or else a new hole is excavated. The wasp deposits a single egg on the spider's body and the burrow is sealed.*

2 **Sting in the tail** *Using her considerable strength, the wasp seizes the spider by a leg and flips it over on its back. Alternatively, she can attack from the side. She injects venom into a soft part of the body, which paralyzes the spider within seconds.*

INSECTS

SPIDERS

LOCUSTS: THE FACTS

HABITAT: **Hot, dry areas**

DIET: **Plant material, particularly grasses**

SIZE: **0.4 inch (10 mm) to 4 inches (100 mm) long**

ILLUSTRATED SPECIES: ***Schistocerca gregaria*** **(Africa, Middle East, and Asia)**

Winged Plague

Locusts

Locust is the name given to a number of species of grasshoppers that, under favorable conditions, form enormous swarms that consume all vegetation in their path. Undoubtedly, the extensive cultivation of crops by humans has encouraged locust plagues. But swarming behavior was part of a locust's natural survival strategy long before the beginning of farming. Locusts cause devastation in Africa, the Middle East, central Asia, and Australia. In North America, the Rocky Mountain locust was responsible for some of the most destructive plagues ever recorded. Strangely, this species has not been sighted since 1902. North and South America still have a number of relatively nondestructive species of locust that may have originated from the desert locust of Africa.

The eighth plague of Egypt
In the past, locust plagues were usually interpreted as divine retribution. This German print from the 1400s shows God sending a plague of locusts to punish the Egyptian Pharaoh for not freeing his Israelite slaves.

Swarm enemies

The desert locust regularly forms plagues in northern and western Africa and can devastate some of the poorest countries in the world. Between 2003 and 2005, swarm after swarm, some as big 43 miles (70 km) long and containing billions of individuals, caused massive crop destruction.

CHANGING FACES

Locusts in small numbers tend to avoid each other. However, when their numbers increase during favorable conditions, they undergo a remarkable change, transforming both their appearance and behavior. These changes are initiated by touch as individuals jostle and bump into each other.

Solitary form

Gregarious form

INSECTS

SPIDERS

Trapdoor Spider

Nature's best booby traps are built by trapdoor spiders. The trap is so cleverly designed that prey passing close by has little chance of escape when the hatch lifts and the spider pounces on it. Trapdoor spiders live in burrows, which they excavate with their fangs and line with silk to strengthen the walls and provide a stable internal climate. Females live for up to 20 years in the same burrow. It takes several years for them to reach adulthood. Males are smaller than females. When they reach maturity, they leave their burrows in search of females and die soon after mating.

TRAPDOOR SPIDER: THE FACTS

HABITAT: **Ground dwelling in burrows**

DIET: **Insects and other invertebrates, small lizards**

SIZE: **1.4 inches (35 mm) (females); 1 inch (25 mm) (males)**

ILLUSTRATED SPECIES: *Myrmekiaphila fluviatilis* **(southeastern United States)**

Trapdoor design *The design of the trapdoor varies from a simple flap of silk to an expertly crafted door made of clay reinforced with silk and complete with a silk hinge. The upper side of the door is usually camouflaged. Some species set up silk trip lines that radiate from the burrow entrance. Other species make do with no door at all.*

Gotcha! *She has the element of surprise on her side. In a flash, the hatch is raised and the spider pounces on its unsuspecting victim, which is quickly killed and dragged into the burrow.*

HIDING HOLE

Trapdoor spiders are preyed upon by natural enemies, including predatory centipedes and parasitic wasps. In response, many trapdoor species have an escape plan. These can include false bottoms to the burrow, emergency side exits, and side shafts that can be closed off by an internal trapdoor.

Race to the top *This trapdoor spider has been alerted to the presence of an intruder. The vibrations tell her that it is the right size for a meal.*

A life underground

The world of the female trapdoor spider is very confined. From the moment she begins construction of her own burrow only briefly does she leave the silk-lined walls of her underground world to ambush prey or to mate. Her awareness of the outside world is limited to the vibrations of animals as they pass by the door to her home. From these signals, she can tell the difference among potential prey, suitor, or predator.

Baby food *A female trapdoor spider deposits her eggs in a silken egg sac within the burrow. Newly hatched spiderlings remain in the burrow for months feasting on meals provided by their mother.*

Development of the bolas

Bolas spiders are members of the orb-weaver spider family. Over time they reduced the typical orb-weaver's web of radial and spiral threads to a single sticky thread. Stages of this reduction can be seen in the webs of other orb-weaver spiders.

Stage 1 *A typical orb-weaver's web is symmetrical and supported at the edges by frame threads.*

Stage 2 *The maker of this web gets by with a triangular web that takes less energy to build.*

Stage 3 *This web is like a ladder with dangling rungs of sticky silk.*

Stage 4 *The bolas spider holds on to the remnant frame threads and dangles a single sticky line to snare its prey.*

Swing and Swat
Bolas Spider

The bolas spider takes its name from a rope-and-ball weapon used by cowboys to entangle the legs of running cattle or game. In the spider's case, the target is a moth and the weapon is a ball of sticky silk on a thread. Bolas spiders hunt by night. They hang from a dragline by their back legs patiently dangling their sticky trap like a rod fisher. When a moth comes close, they vigorously swing the bolas to catch it. The bolas is constructed of a densely folded silk fiber held together in tacky glue and surrounded by a more liquid glue. The liquid penetrates between the scales on the wings and body of the moth and firmly attaches it to the bolas. Bolas spiders increase their chances of a catch by emitting a chemical that mimics the male-attracting scent released by female moths.

Strike one

The female magnificent spider *Ordgarius magnificus* is aptly named for its strikingly colored abdomen. By day, it hides among leaves bound together with silk, and at night it lures male moths toward the dangling bolas. Bolas spiders in the Americas use their front legs to spin the bolas, while those from Australia, like this one, use their second pair of legs.

BOLAS SPIDER: THE FACTS

HABITAT: Trees and tall shrubs

DIET: Moths

SIZE: 0.6 inch (15 mm) long (females); 0.08 inch (2 mm) long (males)

ILLUSTRATED SPECIES: *Ordgarius magnificus* (eastern Australia)

The aquatic arachnid

The diving bell spider's scientific name is *Argyroneta aquatica*. "Argyroneta" means "silvery net," which is what you will see if you spot a diving bell spider's chamber beneath the ripples of a pond.

DIVING BELL SPIDER: THE FACTS

HABITAT: **Ponds, ditches, slow-moving streams, shallow lakes**

DIET: **Aquatic insects, tadpoles, and small fish**

SIZE: **0.5-inch (13-mm) body length**

SCIENTIFIC NAME: *Argyroneta aquatica*

Diving Bell

Spider

Many spiders live near water. Some can even walk on the surface, but only one species spends all of its time underwater. The diving bell spider lives within an air-filled chamber, or bell, beneath the surface of shallow lakes and ponds. To build the bell, the spider first anchors a curved pad of silk to the stems of water plants. It then adds air bubbles transported from the surface. The male is unusual among spiders for being larger than the female. He builds his bell next to a female's and connects it to her bell with a tunnel. After they mate, the female deposits about 50 eggs into an egg sac stored in the roof of her bell.

Surfacing for air *To keep the bell supplied with air, water spiders swim to the surface to trap air bubbles among the hairs surrounding their back legs and abdomen. They release the bubbles when they return to the bell.*

Deadly diver Diving bell spiders prey on any aquatic insects, crustaceans, tadpoles, or fish that come close to their bell. They also go on hunting expeditions, during which they breathe from a thin film of air around their abdomen. They always consume their prey back in the chamber. Diving bell spiders are themselves prey to fish, frogs, and aquatic reptiles.

Eight-legged Leaper
Jumping Spider

Jumping spiders make up by far the largest group of spiders. Instead of using a web to trap prey, they stalk their victims and, when close enough, pounce like a cat. They have powerful back legs and can jump up to 50 times their body length. Jumping spiders are inquisitive creatures that explore their environment and adapt their hunting strategy to the circumstances. Unusual among spiders, they hunt by day. Like all spiders, they use a silk thread that they attach to the ground in case they happen to leap over an edge in pursuit of prey or to escape danger. Jumping spiders have good vision. Males of many species have brightly colored bodies that they display to females during elaborate courtship dances.

JUMPING SPIDER: THE FACTS

HABITAT: **All terrestrial habitats except polar regions**

DIET: **Insects and spiders**

SIZE: **0.08-inch (2-mm) to 0.9-inch (22-mm) body length**

ILLUSTRATED SPECIES: *Evarcha culicivora* (eastern Africa)

Good looker

The large central eyes give sharp telephoto vision (red); the pair of side front eyes give binocular vision for judging distances (orange); and the side eyes give wide angle vision for detecting movement (yellow).

Vampire spider

There is at least one species of spider that has a taste for human blood. Native to the shores of Lake Victoria in Africa, the jumping spider *Evarcha culicivora* uses its keen eyesight to single out mosquitoes that have recently had a meal of blood. They creep up behind their victim and then pounce on its back. The mosquito is quickly paralyzed and the spider sucks the liquid blood from its body.

Eyes all around Jumping spiders have the best vision of all invertebrates. This allows them to identify their prey, stalk it, and calculate their exact trajectory as they leap for the kill. A jumping spider's eyes are in front and to the sides of the head. The large front pair of eyes can zoom in on details in the same way a telephoto camera lens can. These eyes can also detect color.

Insect and Spider
Families

Arthropods

Arthropod species

Insects	90%
Arachnids	5%
Crustaceans	4%
Centipedes/millipedes	1%

Insects

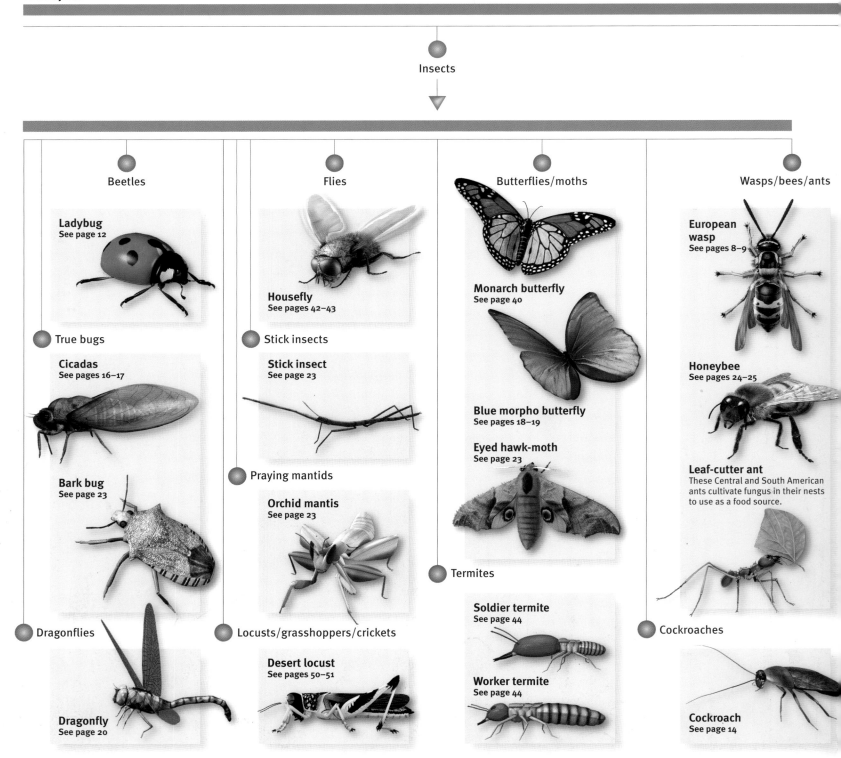

Beetles

Ladybug
See page 12

True bugs

Cicadas
See pages 16–17

Bark bug
See page 23

Dragonflies

Dragonfly
See page 20

Flies

Housefly
See pages 42–43

Stick insects

Stick insect
See page 23

Praying mantids

Orchid mantis
See page 23

Locusts/grasshoppers/crickets

Desert locust
See pages 50–51

Butterflies/moths

Monarch butterfly
See page 40

Blue morpho butterfly
See pages 18–19

Eyed hawk-moth
See page 23

Termites

Soldier termite
See page 44

Worker termite
See page 44

Wasps/bees/ants

European wasp
See pages 8–9

Honeybee
See pages 24–25

Leaf-cutter ant
These Central and South American ants cultivate fungus in their nests to use as a food source.

Cockroaches

Cockroach
See page 14

Classifying arthropods

Species are categorized into groups according to how closely related they are to one another. Members of each group can be identified as such because they share a number of body features. In this way, scientists organize information about the diversity of life.

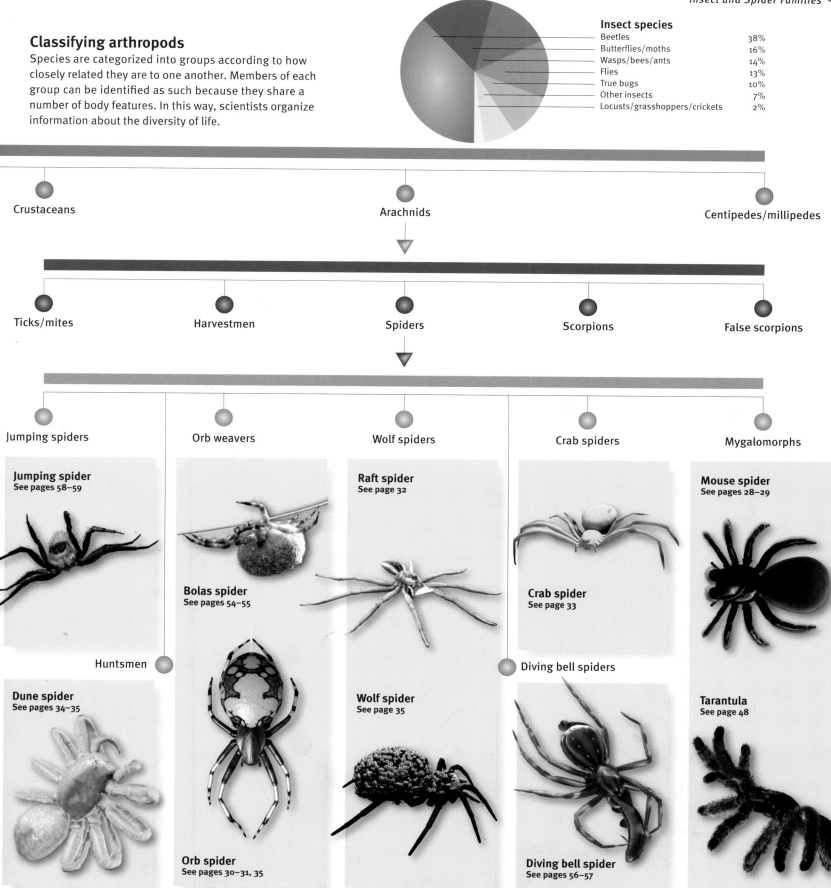

Insect species

Beetles	38%
Butterflies/moths	16%
Wasps/bees/ants	14%
Flies	13%
True bugs	10%
Other insects	7%
Locusts/grasshoppers/crickets	2%

Crustaceans

Arachnids

Centipedes/millipedes

Ticks/mites

Harvestmen

Spiders

Scorpions

False scorpions

Jumping spiders

Orb weavers

Wolf spiders

Crab spiders

Mygalomorphs

Jumping spider
See pages 58–59

Bolas spider
See pages 54–55

Raft spider
See page 32

Crab spider
See page 33

Mouse spider
See pages 28–29

Huntsmen

Diving bell spiders

Dune spider
See pages 34–35

Wolf spider
See page 35

Tarantula
See page 48

Orb spider
See pages 30–31, 35

Diving bell spider
See pages 56–57

Glossary

abdomen In an insect or spider, the rear part of the body. It contains the digestive, respiratory, circulatory, and reproductive organs.

adaptation Changes that occur to a species over thousands or millions of years that help it to survive in a particular habitat. Crab spiders have developed the ability to change color to match the flower they are standing on as an adaptation to ambush prey.

antenna The delicate appendages on an insect's head that an insect uses to smell, touch, or hear. Insects have two antennae, which can be long or short, thin, branched, or feather-like.

arachnid An arthropod with eight legs. Spiders and their relatives—including scorpions, harvestmen, ticks, and mites—are all arachnids.

arthropod An animal with jointed legs and a body divided into segments covered by an exoskeleton. Arthropods are an extremely large and varied group of animals that include insects, spiders, centipedes, millipedes, crabs, and lobsters.

ballooning A method used by juvenile spiders and small adult spiders to travel long distances. They are carried on the wind as they dangle from a long strand of silk.

camouflage Colors and patterns that help disguise an animal so that it blends in with its surrounding environment. Insects and spiders camouflage themselves as leaves, bark, or flowers to avoid being seen by predators or prey or both.

carnivore An animal that feeds on other living animals.

caste A group of individuals in a colony that carry out certain tasks. Termites and wasps, bees, and ants are social insects that live in colonies. The castes include the reproductive individuals, the queen and kings; and the sterile workers and soldiers.

caterpillar The larval stage of butterflies and moths.

cephalothorax The combined head and thorax that forms the front part of a spider. The poison fangs, pedipalps, and eight legs are attached to it. It also holds the spider's brain, venom glands, and a muscular stomach that sucks in fluids.

chitin The light yet tough material that makes up an insect's exoskeleton and wings.

cocoon A protective case, often made of silk. Some insects protect their pupae in a cocoon. Spiders also lay their eggs in a silken cocoon called an egg sac.

colony A group of animals of the same species that live and work together to survive. The inhabitants of an ant nest, termite mound, and beehive are all examples of insect colonies.

complete metamorphosis One of two main ways in which an insect develops into an adult during development. The insect changes from a larva to a pupa to a mature adult. The larva looks very different from the adult and dramatically changes its form in the pupal stage before emerging as the fully developed adult insect.

compound eyes An insect's main pair of eyes, made up of a large number of individual eyes. Compound eyes can distinguish shapes and colors and are particularly sensitive to movement.

dragline An attached thread of silk that a spider trails behind it as it moves around. It is used as a safety line if the spider jumps over an edge or drops out of its web. The spider also uses it as a guide to find its way home.

egg sac A silk covering woven by a female spider to wrap up her eggs to protect them and keep them from drying out.

evolution The gradual change that occurs in organisms over thousands or millions of years as they adapt to changing environments and conditions.

exoskeleton The hard outer skeleton of an arthropod. It is a tough, jointed shell made of chitin and hardened protein that supports the muscles and protects soft internal organs.

gland An organ that produces a secretion, such as venom or silk.

grub The larva of an ant, bee, wasp, or beetle. They are usually legless. Grubs that have legs can look a little like caterpillars.

haltere One of a pair of club-like structures. The halteres are the modified hind wings of flies that allow them to keep their bodies balanced and level during flight.

hibernation The practice of remaining inactive during the cold winter months. Like bears, many insects hibernate, either as eggs, larvae, pupae, or adults.

incomplete metamorphosis One of two main ways in which an insect develops. The juvenile stages are similar in form to the adult and are often called nymphs. The metamorphic change to the adult typically involves wing development as well as sexual maturity.

invertebrate An animal that has no backbone. Some invertebrates, such as worms and jellyfish, have soft bodies, but others, like arthropods, are protected by their hard exoskeletons.

larva The immature stage of insects when they look completely different from their parents. Larvae

must undergo complete metamorphosis to become adults. Caterpillars, maggots, and grubs are larvae.

maggot The legless larva of some flies.

mandibles The jaws of an insect.

metamorphosis The process of changing form during development. Insects develop from young to adults either by complete or incomplete metamorphosis.

migration The traveling of a group of animals from one region to another, usually to breed or to find food at a particular time. Some butterflies travel thousands of miles, while some tiny beetles and springtails will migrate just a few inches to avoid cold soil temperatures.

mimicry An adaptation whereby an animal imitates another animal. Insects and spiders are able to fool attackers into thinking they are dangerous or poisonous when they are not, and thus avoid being eaten.

molt The process of shedding an outer layer of the body. Insects and spiders molt their old exoskeletons as they grow bigger.

nymph The young stages of insects when they look similar to their parents. Nymphs undergo incomplete metamorphosis to become adults without going through a pupal stage.

ocelli Small, light-sensitive eyes. Many insects have three ocelli on the top of their head, which help them stay level in flight or tell nocturnal insects when it is getting dark.

order A large group of related plants or animals. Insects are divided into about 30 different orders, each with certain features in common. Spiders belong to only one order within the arachnids. An order is divided into smaller groups, such as families, genera, and species.

organism Any living creature, animal, plant, fungus, or microbe.

ovipositor A tube at the tip of the abdomen of a female insect used for laying eggs. The ovipositor of a wasp or bee has evolved into a stinger.

parasite An organism that feeds off another organism, called a host, usually without killing the host but still causing it some harm.

pedipalp A spider's sense organ. A spider has two pedipalps at the front of its cephalothorax that it uses to touch, taste, and smell. Male spiders also use modified pedipalps to transfer sperm to the female during mating.

predator An animal that preys on other animals for its food.

prey The animal that forms the diet of a predator.

proboscis The tubelike mouthpart used by many insects to suck up liquid food.

pupa The stage in development that an insect undergoes when metamorphosing to the adult stage. In the pupa the juvenile body parts break down and adult features emerge.

scavenger An animal that feeds on dead organic matter, such as food scraps, corpses, dung, and shed skin.

scientific name The name given by scientists for a particular species. Each species is given two names. The first has a capital letter and both names are printed in italics.

social insect An insect that lives in a colony with other individuals of the same species. They cooperate in caring for the young, maintaining the nest, and finding food. Ants, termites, and some bees and wasps are social insects.

species A group of organisms that have certain features in common and breed only with one another.

spinnerets Two to six finger-like appendages at the tip of a spider's abdomen. Various types of silk made by the spider emerge from the spinnerets.

spigots The individual nozzles at the tips of the spinnerets. As silk emerges from the spigots, it is spun into threads by the spinnerets.

spiracle A breathing hole along the sides of an insect that takes air into the body and expels carbon dioxide. Insects have between two and eleven pairs of spiracles. Spiders also have spiracles leading into their breathing organs.

swarm A mass of insects, such as bees or locusts, that collect and move around together for feeding, mating, or finding a new nest site.

thorax The middle section of an insect's body. It contains the muscles that move the insect's wings and legs.

trachea A breathing tube. Humans and other terrestrial vertebrates have only one trachea, which leads to the lungs. Insects and some spiders have a whole network of tracheae that carry oxygen to all parts of the body.

tympanum A membrane that acts like an ear drum in crickets, grasshoppers, and cicadas. The tympana vibrate when they receive sounds, and this information is carried to the brain via the nervous system so the insect can hear.

venom A chemical that is injected into another animal to kill or paralyze it or to deter it from attacking.

vertebrate An animal that has a backbone, such as fishes, reptiles, birds, and mammals.

Index

Credits

The publisher thanks Alexandra Cooper for her contribution, and Puddingburn for the index.

ILLUSTRATIONS
bcl=bottom center left; bl=bottom left; br=bottom right; c=center; cl=center left; cr=center right; r=right; tr = top right

Front cover Steve Hobbs c; MBA Studios r; **back cover** Leonello Calvetti bl, bc; MBA Studios tr; **spine** MBA Studios

Peter Bull Art Studio 20–1, 22–3; **Leonello Calvetti** 8–9, 24–5, 42–3, 48–9; ***.tina draempaehl** 26–7c, tr; **Christer Eriksson** 10–11, 54–5; **Steve Hobbs** 12–13, 14–15, 16–17, 26b, 40–1, 44–5, 46–7; **MBA Studios** 28–9, 30–1, 32–3, 34–5, 36–7, 50–1, 52–3, 56–7, 58–9; **Jurgen Ziewe (The Art Agency)** 18–19

MAPS
Andrew Davies; Map Illustrations

PHOTOGRAPHS
bcl=bottom center left; bl=bottom left; br=bottom right; c=center; cl=center left; cr=center right; r=right; tr = top right

CBT=Corbis; GI=Getty Images; PL=photolibrary.com

11bcl, cl PL; **16**bl PL; **26**tr CBT; **30**cr PL; **40**bcl, cl PL; **47**br GI; **50**bl PL